Smithsonian

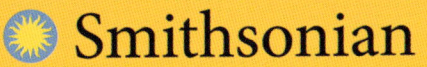

LITTLE EXPLORER

POWERFUL PRAYING MANTISES

by Melissa Higgins

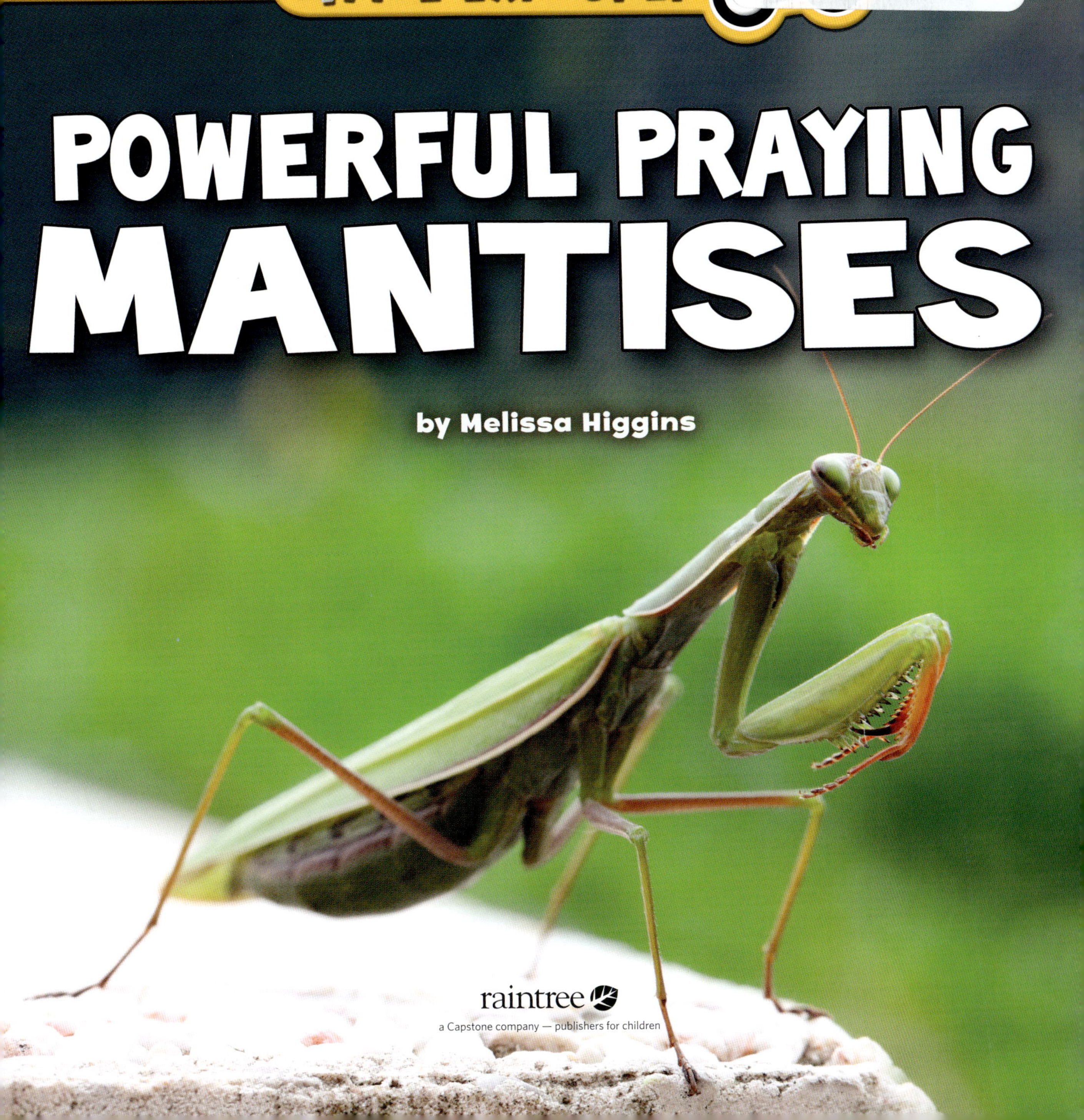

raintree

a Capstone company — publishers for children

Raintree is an imprint of Capstone Global Library Limited, a company incorporated in England and Wales having its registered office at 264 Banbury Road, Oxford, OX2 7DY – Registered company number: 6695582

www.raintree.co.uk
myorders@raintree.co.uk

Text © Capstone Global Library Limited 2021
The moral rights of the proprietor have been asserted.

All rights reserved. No part of this publication may be reproduced in any form or by any means (including photocopying or storing it in any medium by electronic means and whether or not transiently or incidentally to some other use of this publication) without the written permission of the copyright owner, except in accordance with the provisions of the Copyright, Designs and Patents Act 1988 or under the terms of a licence issued by the Copyright Licensing Agency, Barnard's Inn, 86 Fetter Lane, London, EC4A 1EN (www.cla.co.uk). Applications for the copyright owner's written permission should be addressed to the publisher.

Edited by Abby Huff
Designed by Kyle Grenz
Original illustrations © Capstone Global Library Limited 2021
Picture research by Tracy Cummins
Production by Katy LaVigne
Originated by Capstone Global Library Ltd
Printed and bound in India

978 1 4747 9461 9 (hardback)
978 1 4747 9475 6 (paperback)

British Library Cataloguing in Publication Data
A full catalogue record for this book is available from the British Library.

Acknowledgements
We would like to thank the following for permission to reproduce photographs: Alamy: age fotostock, 11 (bottom), Bryan Reynolds, 23, Tim Gainey, 17; iStockphoto: Kaan Sezer, 7 (top), Vince Adam, 9; Shutterstock: Bankim Desai, 7 (middle), Cathy Keifer, 5 (top), 7 (bottom right), 25 (bottom), 29, Chechu de la Fuente, 11 (top), Dave Welch, 13, Eric Isselee, 5 (bottom), 19 (bottom), IamTK, 27, kunchit jantana, 2, Marek R. Swadzba, 7 (bottom left), Melinda Fawver, 25 (middle), Mr. SUTTIPON YAKHAM, 25 (top), Ondrej Prosicky, 21, Patricia Chumillas, 12, Sebastian Janicki, cover, Stubblefield Photography, 15, YSK1, 26, Yzoa, 1, Zaruba Ondrej, 19 (top)

Our very special thanks to Gary Hevel, Public Information Officer (Emeritus), Entomology Department, at the Smithsonian National Museum of Natural History. Capstone would also like to thank Kealy Gordon, Product Development Manager, and the following at Smithsonian Enterprises: Ellen Nanney, Licensing Manager; Brigid Ferraro, Vice President, Education and Consumer Products; and Carol LeBlanc, Senior Vice President, Education and Consumer Products.

Every effort has been made to contact copyright holders of material reproduced in this book. Any omissions will be rectified in subsequent printings if notice is given to the publisher.

All the internet addresses (URLs) given in this book were valid at the time of going to press. However, due to the dynamic nature of the internet, some addresses may have changed, or sites may have changed or ceased to exist since publication. While the author and publisher regret any inconvenience this may cause readers, no responsibility for any such changes can be accepted by either the author or the publisher.

Contents

Gentle or fierce?... 4
Spiny flower mantises 6
Orchid mantises 8
Mediterranean mantises...................... 10
Giant Asian mantises............................. 12
Chinese mantises.................................... 14
Grass mantises... 16
Dead leaf mantises................................ 18
Shield mantises.. 20
Ground mantises..................................... 22
Stick mantises 24
Bark mantises... 26
Unicorn mantises.................................... 28

Glossary... 30
Comprehension questions 31
Find out more... 31
Index..32

Words in **bold** are in the glossary.

Gentle or fierce?

The praying mantis has a gentle name. But this insect is fierce. Its folded front legs quickly snatch **prey**. The legs have long spikes. The spikes hold the mantis's food and don't let it slip away.

Mantises use **camouflage**. The colours and shape of their bodies blend in with where they live. Mantises hide from enemies and surprise prey.

There are about 2,000 known **species** of praying mantises. Most live in warm places.

DID YOU KNOW?

Many people call these insects *mantises*. But another name for them is *mantid*.

A mantis's body

Praying mantises are insects. They have six legs and three body parts. They also have two sets of wings. You can tell a mantis by its long body and bent front legs. Two big eyes give it good vision for hunting.

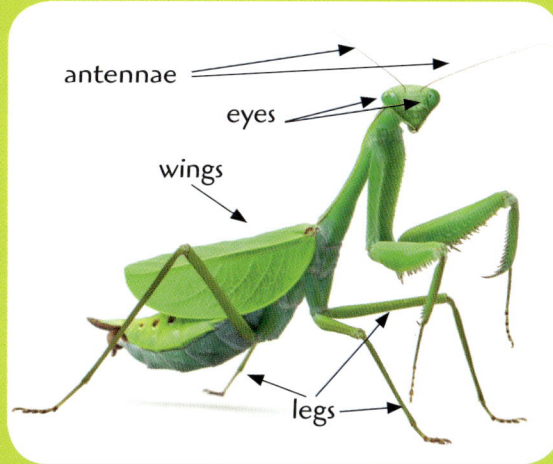

Spiny flower mantises

Found: Africa
Length: 2.5 to 3.8 centimetres (1 to 1.5 inches)

Spiny flower mantises are masters of **disguise**. Two large spots dot each wing. **Predators** think the spots are the eyes of a bigger animal and leave the mantis alone.

Baby spiny flower mantids have a disguise of their own. They look like ants. Their bodies change as they grow. Later, they blend in with flowers or leaves. This keeps them hidden until they grow wings. Then they can fly from danger.

DID YOU KNOW?
Many animals eat mantises, including birds, bats and snakes.

A praying mantis's life

Female mantises lay up to 400 eggs in a watery froth. The froth dries into a hard case. It helps keep the eggs safe. Baby mantises called **nymphs** hatch from the eggs. They look like tiny adults without wings. Nymphs **moult** as they grow into adults. Most live for less than one year.

egg case

adult

nymphs

Orchid mantises

Found: Southeast Asia
Length: 2.5 to 7 cm (1 to 2.75 inches)

A young orchid mantis looks like a flower. Its shape and colour hide it from enemies. But its body also draws in insects. A fly, bee or moth sees the mantis. The insect thinks the mantis's pink legs are the petals of a flower. The insect flies closer to have a look. Then the mantis grabs the insect and eats it.

DID YOU KNOW?

Mantises are meat-eaters. They feed on insects such as flies, crickets and grasshoppers. Big mantises can eat lizards, frogs, snakes, birds and rodents.

Mediterranean mantises

Found: Europe, North America and Western Asia
Length: 6.5 cm (up to 2.5 inches)

A bird hunts for food. It spies a Mediterranean mantis. This mantis does not run. It faces its enemy. It lifts its front legs and raises its wings. The wings have two spots. They look like big eyes. The mantis has another trick to scare away animals. It rubs its hind wings together. They make a loud scraping noise.

DID YOU KNOW?
Praying mantises might look scary, but they are harmless to people. They do not sting or use **venom**.

Looking at you

All mantises can turn their heads 180 degrees. That's a semicircle. They are the only insects that can turn their head so far. This helps them spot food and foes.

Giant Asian mantises

Found: Southeast Asia
Length: 7.6 to 9 cm (3 to 3.5 inches)

The giant Asian mantis is big! It's the size of a human palm. Most mantises wait for food to come to them. Giant Asian mantises hunt. They chase animals up to half their size. Like all mantises, they use **mandibles** to eat. The sharp mouthparts chew and tear.

All mantises have mandibles.

Giant Asian mantises are green, yellow or brown. They can change colour to blend in with their home. Changing colour takes a few days.

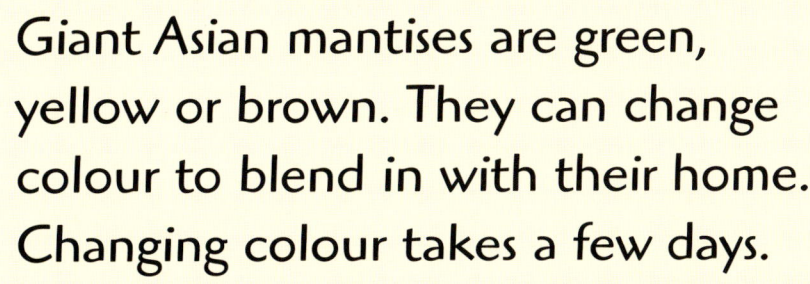

DID YOU KNOW?

Mantises eat each other. Females sometimes eat males after they **mate**. A baby mantis's first meal is often one of its brothers or sisters.

Chinese mantises

Found: Asia, Europe and North America
Length: 5.1 to 12.7 cm (2 to 5 inches)

In the late 1800s, Chinese mantises arrived in the United States on plants that were sent from China. People also bought them to put in their gardens to eat pests. Now, Chinese mantises live across North America and Europe. They are an **invasive species**, which means they spread in ways that are harmful to native plants and animals.

Good or bad for gardens?

Some gardeners like praying mantises. They eat insect pests such as **aphids**. But there is a downside to mantises. They also eat insects that are good for plants, such as moths and butterflies. These insects spread pollen. Plants need pollen to make new plants.

DID YOU KNOW?

Chinese mantises go after big prey. They even eat hummingbirds. At least 12 types of praying mantises eat small birds.

Grass mantises

Found: North America, South America and Southeast Asia
Length: 5.5 to 7 cm (2.2 to 2.75 inches)

Is that a blade of grass? Look closer. It is a grass mantis. Green ones are found in living grass. They blend in. Brown grass mantids live in dry grass and pine needles.

Most mantises mate to make eggs. Some grass mantises are different. The female can make eggs by herself. This is a way some animals have **adapted**. They can survive even if no males are around.

The Indian grass mantis has a very thin body.

DID YOU KNOW?

Male praying mantises often have bigger wings than females. Big wings help them fly to find mates.

Dead leaf mantises

Found: Africa, South America and Southeast Asia
Length: 4.5 to 8.5 cm (1.8 to 3.3 inches)

It's easy to see how the dead leaf mantis got its name. Its brown colours are the same as dead leaves. The edges of its body are bumpy. They look like tiny rips.

One type of dead leaf mantis hangs from a twig. If touched, it sways like a leaf in a breeze. If touched too hard, it drops to the ground. Then watch your step! These mantids blend in with the forest floor.

> **DID YOU KNOW?**
> At least two styles of martial arts are based on the movements of praying mantises.

Batty

Most praying mantises have just one ear. It's found under the belly. It does not hear the sounds human ears do. It hears high-pitched sounds made by bats as they hunt. A mantis's ear warns it to get away from the bat.

ear

Shield mantises

Found: Central and South America
Length: 9 cm (about 3.5 inches)

This green mantis has a large flap behind its head. People say it looks like a shield.

The shield mantis's green body also looks like a leaf. It matches the plants where it lives. This disguise fools prey and predators. Small birds that do spot the shield mantis might not eat it. The mantis's flaps are very wide and are hard to swallow.

DID YOU KNOW?
Mantises strike fast! They grab prey six times faster than humans can blink their eyes.

Shield mantises are also called leaf mantises and hooded mantises.

Ground mantises

Found: North America and Australia
Length: 1 to 3 cm (0.4 to 1.2 inches)

The ground mantis does not wait for prey. It chases food. This small mantis lives on the ground. Its brown body blends in with sand and soil.

The ground mantis quickly runs from danger. It hides under plants. It also protects itself by standing tall and sticking out its arms. This is meant to scare off predators.

Skinner's ground mantis

DID YOU KNOW?

The smallest mantis in the world is a ground mantis. It lives in Australia. It is just 1 cm (0.4 inches) long.

Stick mantises

Found: Africa, Asia, Australia, North America and South America
Length: 7 to 15 cm (2.8 to 6 inches)

Most mantises live in shrubs and trees. So looking like a stick is a good disguise. Some stick mantises are thin. They look like small twigs. Others are thick and look like bumpy wood.

Stick mantises can be very big. The giant African stick mantis grows up to 15.2 cm (6 inches) long. It sits still. It waits for prey to come close enough to grab.

DID YOU KNOW?
Praying mantises eat their prey head first.

The African twig mantis holds out its front legs to look more like a stick.

Praying mantis or stick insect?

It's easy to mistake praying mantises for stick insects. Both are long. They blend in with their **habitats**. How can you tell them apart? Most stick insects have thin heads. Their front legs do not fold up. Praying mantises only eat animals. Stick insects only eat plants.

praying mantis

stick insect

Bark mantises

Found: Central and West Africa, Australia and Southeast Asia
Length: 2 to 4 cm (0.78 to 1.6 inches)

The bark mantis sits on a tree trunk. It has brown, grey and olive stripes. These colours match the tree bark. The mantis also presses its flat body against the tree. Predators find it hard to see the mantis.

DID YOU KNOW?

Baby bark mantises, and many other young mantises, look like black ants. Birds don't like the way the ants taste, so they often leave the young mantises alone.

Most female mantises leave their eggs after laying them. One type of female bark mantis stays with her eggs. She keeps them safe from wasps, ants and beetles.

Unicorn mantises

Found: Southeast Asia, North America and South America
Length: 5 to 9 cm (2 to 3.5 inches)

This mantis has a spike on its head. People think it looks like a unicorn's horn. Scientists are not sure why the mantis has the spike. It looks a bit like a leaf bud or a thorn. The spike might help the mantis to blend in with plants.

Some young unicorn mantises use another disguise. They curl the back part of their bodies. It looks like a **scorpion's** tail. Predators stay away.

Texas unicorn mantis

DID YOU KNOW?

A unicorn mantis really has two spikes. They move close together as the mantid grows.

Glossary

adapt change in order to survive

aphid insect that sucks plant juices

camouflage animal's colouring or shape that helps it to blend in with things around it

disguise animal's colouring or shape that makes it look like something else

habitat natural place or type of place in which a plant or animal lives

invasive species plant or animal that has been brought into a place where it is not naturally found and is spreading in a way that harms native plants or animals

mandibles strong mouthparts used to chew

mate join together and produce young

moult shed an outer layer of skin

nymph young form of an insect

predator animal that hunts other animals for food

prey animal hunted by another animal for food

scorpion animal with a curved tail that has a stinger at the end

species group of living things that can reproduce with one another

venom poisonous liquid made by some animals

Comprehension questions

1. Praying mantises are hunters. What about their bodies make them good at catching prey?
2. If you had insect pests in your garden, would you bring in mantises to help deal with the problem? Why or why not?
3. Pick one praying mantis from this book. How is it different from other mantises?

Find out more

Books

Bugs (DK Find out!), DK (DK Children, 2017)

Insects and Spiders: Explore Nature with Fun Facts and Activities (Nature Explorers), DK (DK Children, 2019)

Praying Mantis vs Giant Hornet: Battle of the Powerful Predators (Minibeast Wars), Alicia Z. Klepeis (Raintree, 2017)

Superstar Insects (Animal Superstars), Louise Spilsbury (Raintree, 2018)

Website

www.dkfindout.com/uk/animals-and-nature/insects/mantises
Find out more about mantises.

Index

adaptations 16
ants 6, 26

bats 19
birds 6, 8, 10, 15, 20, 26
bodies 5

camouflage 4, 6, 13, 16,
    18, 22, 25, 26, 28

disguises 6, 8, 20, 24,
    26, 28

ears 19
eating 8, 12, 14, 24
eggs 7, 16, 27
eyes 5, 6, 10

flowers 6, 8

gardens 14

habitat 25
heads 11
hunting 5, 12, 20, 22

invasive species 14

leaves 6, 18, 20, 28
legs 4, 5, 8, 10, 22
life cycle 7

mandibles 12
mantids 5
mating 13, 16, 17
moulting 7

nymphs 6, 7, 13, 26, 28

plants 14, 20, 22, 25, 28
predators 6, 19, 20, 22,
    26, 27, 28
prey 4, 8, 13, 14, 15,
    20, 22, 24

spikes 4, 28, 29
stick insects 25

venom 10

wings 5, 6, 7, 10, 17
world's smallest mantis 23